MW01200137

High

Performance

Develop Mental Toughness, Boost Willpower, Master New Skills, and Achieve Your Goals Faster

SOM BATHLA

www.sombathla.com

Your Free Gift

As a token of my thanks for taking time out to read my book, I would like to offer you a gift bundle:

You can also download your gift at:
http://sombathla.com/freegiftbundle

More Books by Som Bathla

- Fast Track Your Success

- The Mindful Mind

- Conquer Your Fear Of Failure

- The Mindset Makeover

- Living Beyond Self Doubt

- Focus Mastery

- Just Get It Done

You may also visit all books together at http://sombathla.com/amazon

Table of Contents

Your Free Gift 2

Chapter 1: What is High Performance?...........5

Chapter 2: How the Science of High
Performance Works For Everyone 18

Chapter 3: Self-Image Controls Your
Performance and How to Re-calibrate It?.....30

Chapter 4: Mind Training Techniques To
Develop Mental Toughness..........................43

Chapter 5: Proven Principles To Acquire Any
New Skill Faster 71

Chapter 6: The Science of Expertise – How
Highly Successful Attain Mastery 97

Chapter 7: Key Tenets to Activate High
Performance in Your Everyday Life.............110

Chapter 8: Scientific Ways to Boost Your
Willpower for Sustained Performance........129

Chapter 9: The Neuroscience of Peak
Performance or 'Flow' State & How You Can
Experience It. 151

Closing Thoughts..168

Chapter 1: What is High Performance?

****

"Don't lower your expectations to meet your performance. Raise your level of performance to meet your expectations."

~Ralph Marston

It was not just a regular day at the office for Jenny.

She would finally get to know her performance appraisal results along with other colleagues. Therefore, she was a bit nervous. She was frequently looking at her watch and then towards the cabin of her Marketing Head. The marketing department, she worked in, was buzzing more than usual. Jenny noticed people going in and out of her boss's office. Each colleague was spending *fifteen to twenty* minutes in there.. A few people came out looking cheerful, while others didn't seem that happy – and few seemed frustrated.

Her heart started beating faster, as it was her turn now – she was about to enter that corner room in next ten minutes. We want and keep longing for things in life, but when those moments arrive, we get nervous and full of anxiety. Jenny was experiencing similar thoughts and emotions.

Finally, she was called in. Her reporting manager, a tall handsome man in his early forties sat along with a young HR representative from the organization. Jenny took her seat and after just initial greetings, the discussion on appraisal and feedback started.

She started realizing her anxiety and fears were not unfounded. She got the feedback that her performance was not up to the mark and the organization desired her to gear up faster, strengthen her competencies and skillset to address her job requirements better. Finally, she received a letter that offered an average three-star performance rating (five stars being the top performance) with a marginal salary hike. Deeply sad and frustrated, she came out of the room and managed to reach at her desk.

Sitting at her desk, she started to realize what had happened. She thought about all her colleagues who came out looking happy. Then she thought of Zara. Zara was one of the smartest young women in her marketing team and she had come out of the room with a big victorious smile on her. In next few minutes, Jenny was at Zara's workstation enquiring how Zara's performance was rated by the company. Zara told her about her wonderful performance appraisal, with a promotion to the next level, and a decent pay hike.

After this brief talk with Zara and somehow managing her work during the day, she left early. Sitting at home, Jenny tried to understand what had led to her bad performance rating. She was equally thoughtful and curious to recollect past instances about Zara's stupendous performance. Jenny also recalled that Zara always had enjoyed more freedom in her work, because she had always delivered great results. She was quite independent in her approach of dealing with the organizations' clients and meetings - she enjoyed a great amount of flexibility to accommodate her meeting schedule with clients. Though Zara seemed to be consistently given more work responsibilities, but she never appeared stressed or worried about her work.

Now Jenny started to introspect on her own working life. She realized that she was mostly anxious about work and what her superiors were going to think about her. She was swamped with work – despite having had much less work than Zara. Further, she was almost always the last one to leave office every day.

Jenny was puzzled and curious to know:

- What made Zara deliver such amazing results despite more work under her belt?
- What made Zara work seemingly without any stress?
- Are there any special traits she hadacquired from her parents or had she learnt the formidable qualities by practice?
- Is there some secret recipe that attributes to her stupendous performance that allows her to lead a successful and happy life?

Now, you would agree that it's not only Jenny who thinks of such question. In this modern day highly competitive and demanding world, almost everyone is curiously searching the answers to the above questions.

Like Jenny, most of the people not only in the corporate world but also in business, sports, and other fields scratch their heads to understand what is the secret recipe these high achievers have in every field of life?

What makes some people crush it in every field, while the majority of the population just find themselves struggling hard to get out their mediocre lives?

What makes such people master their body and mind and always seem beaming with grace despite handling high stake responsibilities?

I've always been curious to see people around me who seem to be performing at a much higher level and with a high velocity. In my corporate life, I also found myself in those phases, where I was growing at a much faster pace in terms of learning and financial rewards. At times I find myself introspecting about some of those factors that led me to perform at higher level in those times like my purpose and direction, my mindset and belief system, my practices. Though, I couldn't categorically list down everything together in the form of a recipe that could lead to such performance. However, based on my study of high performers, I saw some principles such high-achievers follow, but these were wisdom nuggets that were bit scattered and disjointed, therefore, it was difficult to put to use effectively to get the full benefits. The underlying question behind all my research was:

How come someone would attain that state, where he is able to consistently and over a long period of time perform better and deliver high quality results?

If you are like me, I am sure you are also looking for answer to the above question.

I can assure you that you are standing at the right spot now to get the answers to that question. I have written this book specifically with this objective in mind. The book goes deeper into scientific studies and psychological researches and states the principles of high performance by ultra-achievers in different fields of life. These principles have been implemented by successful people in all fields of life, be it sports, arts, or business to deliver the performance at highest level and for a longer sustainable period.

It might be that some people would have accidently applied the principles of high performance at some phase of their life and had seen good results for that period. Even that's a good thing because they have at least tasted the flavor of high performance for some time. But, the objective of this book is to list down the theories and principles in detail, and to understand how they work. Once you understand and then implement these principles in any area of your life, you will know beforehand that you will have benefitted by applying the principles and not by mere random use of tactics. This book is about the long-term strategies that talk about your inner mindset, the science of how your body and mind works, and how you can start applying the principles as you read them. This book is not about some quick tips or tactics with short-lived performance boosts, rather it focuses on a long-term sustainable approach of changing your mindset and presenting a different way of performing your tasks and start achieving success.

Before we dive deep into the principles of achieving the state of high performance; let's first start with your understanding of high performance.

What is High Performance?

The Cambridge dictionary defines High Performance **as the ability to operate to a high standard and at a high speed.**

Take another definition from the Collins Dictionary[1]. It defines high performance by referring to a high-performance car or other product that goes very fast or does

---

[1]
https://www.collinsdictionary.com/dictionary/english/high-performance

a lot. Then it finally puts the general definition as **very efficient and powerful.**

I resonate with the definition of high performance by Brendon Burchard that states: **"high performance is consistently performing and delivering results above and beyond standard norms over the long-term."**

The central theme of all the above definitions is that to deliver a high-performance you must have these pre-requisites:

a. One has to deliver beyond the regular standards i.e., at a standard much higher than the normal.
b. The results should be delivered in a faster way.
c. And lastly, one should be able to deliver such results over the long term on a consistent basis.

Who am I to talk about high performance?

If this is the first book of mine that you've, let me briefly introduce myself. I had been in the corporate world for over seventeen years and since last year, I have become an author. It was my drive and eagerness to accept new challenges that made me start this exciting journey of turning my intangible ideas in the form of tangible words. I have so far authored ten books on personal development, shattering old mindset and beliefs, and improving performance in all areas of life, and with the love of readers like you, multiple books have already hit #1 bestseller at Amazon.

Now coming to the question: what makes me eligible to write a book on this universal quest of achieving the state of high performance? I have had few experiences in my life where I have pretty effectively handled my job assignments, completed them in a short time frame, and earned accolades for that. Outside the business world, I took a physical health challenge to run ten kilometers at a stretch within a period of twelve weeks. It doesn't seem that great an achievement, because we all know people, who have already run multiple marathon races. But why I found this special to mention here that because at the time I took this challenge, I was a little overweight and not physically active; even jogging for half a kilometer seemed like a mega-project to me. But I took the challenge to see if I could cross my falsely created physical and mental limits. Yes, it was such a great feeling when I physically overcame this overwhelming mental threshold limit.

I had been wondering for quite some time about how someone could remain in the state of high performance on demand. I was curious to know how people maintain consistent levels of performance at higher standards, and thus achieve greater success in life. This quest led me to read many books, blogs, to listen to many interviews. While exploring and learning these principles, I implemented a few principles that worked for me.

Through this book, I will share those principles, along with some real-life examples of high achievers. I assure you that by the time you read and put the book down, your mind will have already digested some mental principles that will help you to trigger the next action. Once you implement these principles in your life, you are definitely going to enhance your performance muscles and progress faster towards your highest goals.

With that assurance, I ask you to join this short journey of learning the tools of high performance to improve your life.

Let's get started.

Chapter 2: How the Science of High Performance Works For Everyone

****

"We must believe that we are gifted for something, and that this thing, at whatever cost, must be attained."

— Marie Curie

You might have heard people raving about someone; saying that he or she is gifted with some talent. A vast majority of people still think that all the high-achievers have attained such abilities naturally. With that thought and reasoning, they rule out our possibilities of performing at those levels and achieving that kind of success. What happens next? This majority doesn't try something new or different, relying on their false beliefs. The reason they attribute for not trying is that a few selected people are gifted, but they are not - so why make an effort and waste time in that area?

But if you ever try to explore further about the lives of those high achievers, who you think have succeeded because they had natural abilities or gifts, you will be surprised to know that that most of these people have spent significant parts of their lives developing their competencies and skills. Such people have dedicated themselves to intensive training that drives changes in the brain (and sometimes, depending on the ability, in the body) that make it possible for them to do things that they otherwise wouldn't have been able to do.

Of course it is not possible to change everything, if that relates to some genetic constraints. You cannot expect a five foot person to master the game of basketball, as you would obviously be at a disadvantage while contesting against taller players. Similarly, you cannot expect a super tall woman to be able to comfortably master the game of gymnastics.

But barring those genetic constraints, for most part, the human body and mind can be very well stated as a normalizing machine. If you expose human beings to a different set of environments or circumstances, they have some initial resistance, but over a period of time, the new environment starts appearing normal. Our mind tends to get normalized to the new environment.

Let's understand this with the help of an example. Assume you are an overweight person. If you start going to gym for an hour a day every morning or evening, you will see and meet people who are physically fit and have optimal weight. Initially, you may be reluctant to run the treadmill or pick up the weight, but over time you start getting acclimatized with the new environment. Now if you continue in that environment for some time, you will start getting inspired by the healthy and fit people around you. Suddenly losing weight, which seemed a difficult task earlier, now seems to be within reach, thanks to your exposure to the new environment.

This concept of normalization of human beings is one of the most important features of human ability. Once you are convinced about this feature, you would not simply rule out the door of any possibility for you by naming it as luck or inborn talent.

What are the scientific principles beneath this innate human capacity of adaptation?

Precisely, the principles of homeostasis and neuroplasticity are responsible for this human adaptability. Let's understand these principles one by one.

Homeostasis: Our bodies can adapt to anything

Homeostasis is a key concept in understanding how our body works. It is formed with two Greek words: 'homeo,' meaning 'similar,' and 'stasis,' meaning 'stable.' A more formal definition of homeostasis is a characteristic of a system that regulates its internal environment and tends to maintain a stable, relatively constant, condition of properties.

Homeostasis means a system's tendency to do what it needs to do to maintain stability. We are talking about a system of our body and mind. Every cell in our body and brain is *constantly* working to maintain a sense of stability—adjusting everything from our blood pressure and heart rate to our pH balance and blood sugar levels. Our body wants to keep things stable and normal at a particular level all the time.

Therefore, whenever we push ourselves beyond what is comfortable for our bodies, our bodies respond by overcompensating in the pursuit of creating a new higher level of homeostasis.

That's the reason that any kind of physical activity creates changes in the body: when a body system—certain muscles, the cardiovascular system, or something else— is stressed to the point that homeostasis can no longer be maintained, the body responds with changes that are intended to re-establish homeostasis.

For example, if you start lifting weights at the gym more than you regularly do, your body will ask you, *"What are you doing? You're pushing me out of homeostasis. Let me see what I can do to handle this new load and calibrate a new level of homeostasis."*

The law of homeostasis applies everywhere; it applies to running more miles as compared to the previous day, learning a new language, playing guitar or anything. You have an existing level of comfort or skill or stability in what you do. Whenever you do something new, your body and mind improves its homeostasis and establishes a new standard.

Let's talk about another concept related to human brains:

Neuroplasticity-

The concept of neuroplasticity is all about the plasticity of our minds. Neuroscience has proven that our brains are malleable and can be molded into entirely something different.

Neuroplasticity is an umbrella term referring to the ability of your brain to reorganize itself, both physically and functionally, throughout your life due to your environment, behavior, thinking, and emotions. Science has proven that radical improvements in cognitive function — how we learn, think, perceive, and remember — are possible even in the elderly; these changes can happen regardless of age.

The good news is that your brain makes

physical changes based on the repetitive things you do and experiences you have. The bad news is that your brain makes physical changes based on the repetitive things you do and experiences you have. Therefore, this morphing capability of your brain, known as neuroplasticity, works both for you and against you. In my book *The Mindset Makeover*, I have explained in greater detail the concept of neuroplasticity supported by various studies, and how one can literally change his brain structure and the approach of thinking.

This is a really an exciting feature of the human body and brain. In fact, it's our greatest gift. We need to use it wisely, as we can stretch ourselves beyond our falsely set up mental thresholds that has kept us under certain levels so far.

In fact, the principles of homeostasis and neuroplasticity give us the solid proof that human capability are not fixed or established by the time of our birth. They prove that regardless of whatever environment, we are born and brought up, irrespective of the parents, teachers, friends, we have got in our life, there is always a possibility of stretching and moving beyond what you are.

Believe me, you and I would not be the first one on this crazy journey, if we stretch our abilities and reach to the heights that our hearts have been longing for. You would want to see some examples of the adaptability of human beings, so let's look at few:

This amazing story, rather let me call it, a survival tale of a Swedish adventurer Goran Kropp. In October 1995, this man started his journey from Stockholm, Sweden, on his bicycle. He rode all the way and reached at the base of Himalayas in April 1996. He didn't take any oxygen mask with him, nor did he have the help of any of the sherpas (the local people who know the mountain routes well and accompany the mountaineers). Hence, without oxygen mask and without any other person's help, this brave man reached the summit of Mount Everest on his own. After touching the apex of mountain, he then descended normally and picked up his bike and peddled back to Sweden.

Although this would definitely seem a life-threatening adventure for anyone, but Kropp did this. While reading his adventure, it appeared to me that he did this most difficult job with such an ease that it sounds like going to a supermarket, grabbing your groceries, and coming home. Doesn't it?

That's the power of the adaptability of our bodies and minds.

Let's take another example of the adaptability and limitless of the human potential. If anyone asks you how many miles someone can run in one stretch, some of you may guess about a marathon's length or may be little longer. Remember, I am talking about running in one single stretch without taking any breaks.

You will again be shocked to know that *The Tarahumara*, who are the Native American people of north-western Mexico that can run up to a massive two hundred miles.

Isn't that simply amazing? Two-hundred miles at a stretch!

The above stories prove that human body and minds are highly adaptable. Therefore, you must realize that there is no shortage of our capabilities. We have just believed too much our doubts and negative thinking amassed from our surroundings. One has to take an entirely different approach to seek the benefit of the concept of homeostasis and neuroplasticity. The above examples are the extreme ones, but definitely give the strong message about the limitlessness of the human potential. So, we need to remove the limiting beliefs, rise above our fears and get ready to perform to the best of our abilities.

With deliberate practice, the objective is not merely to reach your potential but to build it, to make things possible that were not possible before. This requires challenging homeostasis—frequently coming out of your comfort zone—and forcing your brain or your body to adapt. But once you do this, learning becomes a way of taking control of your life and shaping your potential in ways that you want to.

Your upper limits are unknown and unknowable. Only, you can go further and test out your limits, no one else. Therefore, you need to take the next step towards the summit of your mountain by getting out of your comfort zone and putting the power of ADAPTABILITY to work.

With that, let's move further.

Chapter 3: Self-Image Controls Your Performance and How to Re-calibrate It?

****

"A strong positive self-image is the best possible preparation for success in life."

– Dr. Joyce Brothers

In the previous section, you learned about the adaptability of human body and brain by the principles of homeostasis and neuroplasticity. Once you understand that you don't have any limits, rather you limit yourself by the false limits created by you and only you, it gives you a sense of liberation.

One more point before we get into learning the specific scientific principles and strategies towards high performance. Here I would like you to spend some time to learn something about your self-image. Because, our self-image plays a vital role in how we approach towards any activity. So, the question arises is how does self-image affect our performance; and can we change our self-image to improve our performance? Let's get straight into that:

There is a broader term known as Self-Concept and one of the subsets of that is Self-Image. Carl Rogers, an American psychologist believes that the self-concept has three different components:

- The view you have of yourself (self-image)
- How much value you place on yourself (self-esteem or self-worth)
- What you wish you were really like (ideal self)

Here we will talk only about self-image. The broad idea about self-image in relation to our discussions on high performance is that your level of performance will be limited to the level, you see yourself as capable of. You would never perform beyond what you see yourself.

Jason Selk, one of the premier performance coaches in United States defines self-image as below:

"Self-image is essentially how you view yourself—what strengths and weaknesses you believe you possess and what you believe you are capable of achieving."

Jason compares your self-image to thermostat and explains how your performance can never exceed the self-image you have set for yourself. In one of his books, he states:

> Essentially, the self-image governs how successful any individual becomes because it motivates and shapes work ethic and effort. In this way, self-image is like a thermostat.

If you set the thermostat at 72 degrees Fahrenheit and the room drops to 71 degrees, the thermostat then sends a message to the heater to get to work. Warm air rushes into the room, and the room warms up to 72 degrees. When the room reaches 73 degrees, the thermostat tells the heater to stop working. All day long, the thermostat governs the temperature in the room and won't allow the room temperature to rise or drop from the desired temperature for long.

Human beings are the same way: we neither outperform nor underperform our self-image for long. That's why it is so important to set your self-image gauge high enough to achieve your life goals. Set your self-image gauge too low, and by definition, you'll underachieve, because your mind won't call for the motivation to achieve more.

Therefore, it becomes even more important to first take a close look at how we see ourselves. Once we are able to see ourselves as capable to do a particular task, then our action will be aligned with our identity. someone rightly stated once: *"Your Identity precedes Activity"*.

How to ascertain your self-image?

If you have some difficulty in identifying your true self-image, thankfully there are some tools that can hold your hand and lead you to the relevant questions that will help you determine your self-image.

In 1954, Manfred Kuhn, a social psychologist, developed a tool known as *The Twenty Statements Test (TST)*[2] that he used to investigate further into the self-image of the people. He asked people to

---

2

http://psychology.wikia.com/wiki/Twenty_Statements_Test

answer the question 'Who am I?' in 20 different ways. He found that the responses could be divided into two major groups. These were *social roles* (external or objective aspects of oneself such as son, teacher, friend) and *personality traits* (internal or affective aspects of oneself such as sympathetic, impatient, humorous).

The list of answers to the question "Who Am I?" includes examples of each of the following four types of responses:

1. **Physical Description**: I'm tall, have blue eyes...etc.

2. **Social Roles:** We are all social beings whose behavior is shaped to some extent by the roles we play. Such roles as being a student, housewife, or member of any sports team not only help others to recognize us, but at the same time,

these roles help us to know what is expected of us in various situations.

3. **Personal Traits:** This is another dimension of our self-description. You might give your personal traits like "I'm impulsive...I'm generous...I tend to worry a lot".

4. **Existential Statements** (abstract ones): These can range from "I'm a child of the universe" to "I'm a human being" to "I'm a spiritual being"...etc.

Depending upon your age, social connections, relationships, and your behaviors, your answers to these questions will vary. You will realize that answering these questions will help you to see your self-image in a broader sense – and that realization itself makes you understand why you perform a particular task in your own way or avoid doing that act.

Take an example: If your self-image whispers in your head, "I am shy guy". Now, you can easily imagine how your behavior would be if you have to attend a party. Your first thought will be to find an excuse not to go. And even if you end up reaching the party, you will stand in a corner and do your best to find a way to get out of the place, as soon as you can. That's the power of self-image, which governs all your behaviors and actions in any particular situation.

Okay, what should we do next?

I suggest spending some time in introspection to assess how you perceive your self-image? Also, don't assume that your self-image is the same throughout your entire life. It is rather fluid and keeps on changing subtly and gradually as you grow up and get exposed to different types of environments. If you think that it is your self-image that is not supporting you to deliver high-performance in your pursuits, then it is time to change your self-image.

How do you change your self-image to perform better?

Yes, it is quite possible. Rather, it can be stated with certainty that everything changes. You have learned already the concepts of homeostasis and neuroplasticity that support the idea that your body and brain changes.

I heard a wonderful quote or saying somewhere. It goes like this: ***"There is only one thing that is constant in life – and that's called 'change'"***

Therefore, coming back to our point of changing of self-image, good part is that it is not that hard to change your self-image. The principles through which your current self-image is formed, do work the same way, when you want to change them for good. The only difference is that earlier you allowed your self-image to build on its own (thanks to outside exposures)– and now you have to control the way, you want to mold your self-image.

Lanny Bassham, an American sports shooter, an Olympics gold medalist, in his book gives his personal example and suggests the ways through which one can change his self-image. Lanny claims to have spoken to hundreds of Olympic athletes and PGA tour pros about their secrets of high performance. And every one of them had answered unequivocally that at least 90% of their game was a mental game.

Therefore, his formula for changing your self-image is through mental training. This mental training serves the dual purpose. First, the practice involves personal statements to see you as an achiever, and secondly the most important is about mentally practicing the performance at the highest level. His mental training formula that serves this dual objective has two components:

1. Mental Rehearsal

This mental rehearsal in not like your vision boards showing the marvelous outcomes like plush dream homes, fancy cars, or foreign travels, etc. It is not about the visualization of you already having achieved the results. It is about the process of taking action towards getting the results. In this approach, you mentally do the rehearsal of performing that task in most effective way and see yourself making the perfect move and see yourself succeeding always.

To this element of mental rehearsal, you need to combine the below personal statement.

2. **A personal statement:** *"I do it all the time"* + *"That's Like me"*

Now, this personal statement is a game changer. These statements do the job of imprinting your new identity of high performance in your brain. This is not some mystical statement. It is based on neuroscience and more specifically the concept of neuroplasticity is based on this principle that our minds get molded depending upon the environment, behavior, thinking, and emotions.

In his book, *With Winning In Mind: The Mental Management System,* Lanny shares his personal example of how only with the help of the mental training as explained above - without putting much physical training, he was able to win the sports. He states that before he won the Olympic gold, he was in the Army. He was stationed somewhere two hundred and fifty miles away from a shooting range. So, in those two years, he was only able to actually shoot for six days and those were during competitions—three days for one national competition and three days for another.

He explains that after his family went to bed, he'd spend two to four hours a night, five nights a week, imagining he was shooting. In this mental rehearsal, he practiced in his mind precisely that he was standing in the correct posture, aiming the point and then final shooting exactly at the destination. And surprisingly, he won both of those national competitions with the help of these mental rehearsals.

That's the power of building a performers self-image clubbed with a mental rehearsal of your best performance.

With that now let's get into tools and strategies that will pave your way to perform at your best in the next chapter onwards.

Chapter 4: Mind Training Techniques To Develop Mental Toughness

****

"You have to train your brain to be positive just like you work out your body."

~ Shawn Achor

If you are not aware, it is important to make a note that our brains are wired psychologically to be negativity biased. Negativity bias[3] implies a behavior that despite carrying equal intensity, things of a more negative nature (e.g. unpleasant thoughts, emotions, or social interactions; harmful/traumatic events) have a greater effect on one's psychological state and processes as compared to neutral or

---

[3] https://en.wikipedia.org/wiki/Negativity_bias

positive things. In other words, something positive will generally have less of an impact on a person's behavior and cognition than something equally emotional but negative.

What this means for us is if we don't voluntarily control our thoughts and emotions, these tiny invisible creatures carry a huge power to ruin our mental state – thus generating a negative behavior resulting into non-performance or performance at a low or below average level.

But, don't come to any conclusions immediately, because the best part is that humans are gifted with consciousness (unlike other animals). We have the power to exercise control on our thoughts, though most people rarely do anything to change the direction of their thoughts - they think that they have no choice, but to float with whatever thought that comes to their head. Only a very small percentage of population, who are growth-oriented, and are sincere about performing to their best of potential, choose to control their thoughts.

In this section, you will learn about few mental shifts or let's call it transforming your thinking patterns - that will help you to overcome your negativity bias to a large extent, if you put sincere efforts into training your mind. Why I call them mental shifts, and not merely changes, is because a shift means a major transformation and not some minor tweak or modification. These mental shifts, backed by studies and experiments by psychology researchers, have the potential to rewire your thinking patterns, which leads to the right set of emotions. And guess what happens? You will start getting amazing results now.

So, let's get straight into these techniques to develop your mental toughness.

1. Take Stress as a Challenge; not a Threat

There is no denying that most people view stress as a threat. They think stress is something they should avoid. But that's not the way high performers look at stress. All successful people, who perform at a high level, look at stress as a challenge. Try to imagine any successful person in your head and you will re-confirm yourself the accuracy of above statement. High-achievers don't get threatened, rather they feel challenged.

Hans Selye, an Austrian endocrinologist, who is known for important scientific work on the hypothetical non-specific response of an organism to stressors and the effects of stress on human body, coined a term "**Eustress**". This term consists of the Greek prefix 'Eu' that means good. Therefore, Eustress means a good or beneficial stress.

If you start to observe your stress as a challenge, then you are giving it the form of EuStress. Researchers call this response a *challenge response*, which is characterized by viewing stress as something positive and therefore it becomes a growth stimulus. In the midst of stress, people who demonstrate the challenge response; do focus proactively on the things that they can control. With that shift in focus on what you can control, your mind produces the required emotions and behavior, thus prompts you to take the required action to take charge of the situation. This also makes you at peace with the things that are out of your control, and reduces unnecessary worry and anxiety.

Let's look at some science behind how this change in perspective towards stress changes the brain chemistry.

Science states that when someone is under stress, the mind needs to release more of DHEA (Dehydroepiandrosterone), a hormone. DHEA is classified as a neurosteroid; in the same way that steroids help your body grow stronger from physical exercise, DHEA helps your brain grow stronger from psychological challenges. Now the key point to note is if you view stress as a challenge and want to face it, then you will get a supply of DHEA from your brain. However, if you think of stress as a threat your mind will release another chemical called cortisol, a stress hormone.

The ratio of DHEA to cortisol that you release during stress is sometimes referred to as the *growth index*[4] of your stress response. A higher growth index — meaning more DHEA relative to cortisol — is associated with thriving during and after stressful experiences. Those who view stress as a challenge and not as a threat have this optimal ratio.

There was a study conducted on the swimmers by dividing into two different groups and see how these two groups consider stress i.e. challenge or threat. The result of study showed that the non-elites viewed stress as something to avoid, ignore, and try to quiet. They felt stress would hurt their performance. The elites, on the other

---

4

http://onlinelibrary.wiley.com/doi/10.1111/j.1540-4560.1998.tb01220.x/abstract

hand, interpreted the stress and the sensations that came with it as an aid to their performance; it prepared them to get the most out of their bodies.

Studies[5] confirm that viewing a stressful situation as an opportunity to improve your skills, knowledge or strengths makes it more likely that you will experience stress inoculation or stress-related growth. Once you appreciate that going through stress makes you better at it, it gets easier to face each new challenge. And the expectation of growth sends a signal to your brain and body: get ready to learn something, because you can handle this.

Work With Stress:

Dr. Robert Eliot in his book *Dare To Be 100* suggests that one should rather work with stress instead of running away from it. He states that the central ingredient in building a familiarity with stress is your own perspective to it. If you view every

---

[5] https://www.ncbi.nlm.nih.gov/pubmed/23478676

miniature departure from your routine environment as a threat of major consequence, then life is going to be really tough for you. Stress expert Eliot advises two things:

"First, don't sweat the little things, and second, everything is a little thing."

You would say that it is easier said than done. But above statement is a fact, which you might have already experienced in your life. For a moment, imagine looking back on your life and identify a few things that had kept you awake. You would realize that in almost all such cases, they have been non-significant today. Take any example of when you have been worried, when you are searching for your first job or setting up your first business or finding your life partner, those events seemed stressful, but today, if you look back, you would think it wasn't that scary.

Dale Carnegie's Four Step Stress-busting Formula

This is the age of getting results at lightning speed. We want quick solutions. Thankfully there is a formula for dealing with stress as well. Dale Carnegie gave straight-forward advice on how to deal with stress through a four-step formula. Here is what he offered to us:

> Experience has proved to me, time after time, the enormous value of arriving at a decision. It is the failure to arrive at a fixed purpose, the inability to stop going around and round in maddening circles - that drives men to nervous breakdowns and living hells. I find that fifty percent of my worries vanishes once I arrive at a clear, definite decision; and another forty percent usually vanishes once I start to carry out that decision.
>
> So, I banish about ninety per cent of my worries by taking these four steps:

1. Writing down precisely what I am worried about.

2. Writing down what I can do about it.

3. Deciding what to do.

4. Starting immediately to carry out that decision.

Therefore, don't get stressed, rather work with stress. Take stress as a challenge to steal the benefits of neurochemistry with the help of right hormones and probably, Carnegie's formula puts it in more simple terms to help you make this mental shift.

With that let's move to the next mental shift.

2. Consistent Thought Replacement

Take any area of your life, where you want to excel in your performance, you will realize that the people you are competing with are equally qualified with the required skill set to deliver the performance.

Take the corporate world, you will find most people possess the requisite qualifications, experience, and necessary skill sets to deliver the job. Rather these factors are the primary criteria for any organization before hiring any person for a particular position. In the world of sports, most of the athletes go through an almost similar set of physical training, diets, or exercising schedule, as others do. Or when you think of any other field of your life, you will realize that the threshold qualifications, skill sets, and experience almost lie in the similar range, when we compare different people.

But then only a handful people out of those can excel and demonstrate their excellence by their performance. You must have wondered, 'Why is it so?"

The answer lies in: They train their mind to choose the most helpful thought in any particular moment. Jason Selk, a performance coach in the US, in his book *10-Minutes Toughness- The Mental*

Training Program for Winning Before the Game Begins, talks about the level of efficiency at which high performers observe and choose their thoughts. He goes on to explain that any given point of time, you have to consistently keep weighing whether the thoughts going on in your mind are supporting your performance or hurting it. In his words:

> If you determine what you want to accomplish in any given situation <u>then lock your mind on what it takes to achieve that goal, you will have a much better chance of reaping the rewards</u>.
>
> This is true in any setting—business, sport, or even social. As often as possible, choose to think about the path to success rather than the obstacles in your way. You have to decide what you want and then put your energy into acquiring it. Don't wait for good luck to find you. Go out and create your luck. The only

reliable method for overcoming self-doubt and negative thinking is to supply something else for your mind to process. In my opinion, the essence of mental toughness is the ability to replace negative thinking with thoughts that are centered on performance cues or that contribute to improved self-confidence.

Therefore, the key tenet of the concept of thought replacement is <u>to consistently observe your thoughts, and always direct your thoughts towards your desired goal</u> and don't let it wander with some negative thoughts or criticism or mere distractions.

You already know that in any sports, the difference between a winner and the first runner-up is so thin. In the business world the executives have to make high stake decisions at a much faster pace. In such high-stake situations, the way you control and replace your thoughts on what is important for your goal, ultimately drives your performance.

The central theme of any kind of approach for training your mind is that you can do it only in the present moment. You cannot take any decisions in the past; nor can you do something in the future. It is only the present moment where you can direct your mind to take any action. Every moment, you have to take some decisions, which carry with them the power to make or mar your progress. Therefore, you need to consciously observe your thoughts from moment to moment, check the quality of those thoughts and if needed, keep supplying your mind with thoughts that will drive you closer to your goals.

3. Master the Moments between Stimulus and Response

There is one higher level of mental training, which is just one level next to observing and replacing the thoughts. In the thought replacement training, you only deal with yourself, your own mind. You control the way it thinks and choose such thoughts that are most beneficial to reach your goals.

But the reality of life is that you do not get distracting or negative thoughts soley from your own mind. It is more often that you have to deal with outside stimulants that trigger your emotions. There can be some person or circumstance outside on which you don't have direct control (unlike the way you can control your mind), which can disturb your mental state and thus adversely affect your performance. Now you have to choose an optimal response for that trigger, in a way that doesn't affect your performance.

In your inner battle, you have to control your own mind and replace your ongoing thoughts. But for this outer world battle, which has a trigger your circumstances and events outside of you, generally most people have some abrupt response that can generally have far-reaching adverse ramifications, if not chosen well.

In stimulus and response mental training you need to keep in your mind that there is always a moment between the stimulus and response. There is some tiny space between when the stimulus hits you and you respond to that trigger. In that space, if you train your mind to listen to the inner cues during that tiny space, you will get the right response that will best serve you.

You can see plenty of examples in real life as well. For instance, you would have seen in sports like soccer that sometimes a player intentionally pushes another person to the side in violation of rules. Here the innocent player, who gets hurt or distracted, has got a stimulus to immediately react. There are two responses options this person has now. The instant react in the spur of the moment will be to hurt the defaulting player in return – that can harm this good player and now both players may get a warning from the referee. There could be a second thoughtful reaction

– to let the referee intervene, which can help the innocent player to focus his thoughts on the game, and let the culprit player be appropriately handled by the referee.

Like the thought replacement training, in case of the outside stimulus also, though it starts from something outside of your mind, would ultimately require you to mindfully choose a response that keeps you on your track towards your purpose. The only additional point to remember here is to realize that there is always some space between the outside stimuli, and the response to be chosen by you.

Take a real-life example:

Assume you are driving on a busy road. On a cross road, another car touches yours and your vehicle gets some scratches. Here, you have got a stimulus from outside –now you have to choose a response. There could be two alternatives, as you would have rightly guessed by now. One - that most often people do – get out of car and start shouting and blaming each other for this fender-bender. What happens next is you get entangled in a fight and spoil your mood – and it ruins your whole day.

Take another alternative: Instead of reacting immediately like in the first scenario, you realized that there is a space before you react. Most people don't realize that there could be any response between the stimulus and reaction. But that's what this mental training is all about. You pause, park your car on the side and ask the other person to park on the side. Both of you are now are out of your vehicles. At this stage, you already know whether this tiny accident was entirely the other person's fault, or you also had some role in that. But whatever it is; your car is already damaged now. If you think that it was entirely the other person's fault, then you will simply ask him to pay for compensation for the damage. If it is the other persons' fault, then in most cases, the other side will get ready for whatever he can to compensate you. If he doesn't agree, then you have now again to think how much the damage is? Does it make sense to call the traffic police and lodge a complaint etc. or just move on? If you were heading towards an important meeting and this is a minor damage, then the mental space that you now have realized after the trigger of stimulus will guide you to just ignore this as a small issue and move on towards your meeting.

In his book Man's Search for Meaning, neurologist Viktor Frankl famously described it this way: **'Between stimulus and response there is a space. In that space is our power to choose our response. In our response lies our growth and our freedom.'"**

The more we are able to practice responding to any stimulus by getting into that spaces, better will be our decision in those moments. And better decisions equal a better life, as rightly summed up in the quote below:

"It Is in Your Moments of Decision That Your Destiny Is Shaped " ~ Tony Robbins

Therefore, performing at higher levels in a sustainable manner for long period of time requires consistent observation and training of your mind. Above mental techniques can be developed through enhancing your inner awareness and adopting any kind of mindfulness practice in your daily routine can offer you right solutions. In my book *The Mindful Mind*, you can find detailed scientific studies and research showing the benefits of mindfulness on your overall brain and body performance, and how you can get started immediately with mindfulness practice.

4. Avoid Mind Pollution to strengthen Mental Muscles

Our conscious brain has a limited span of attention, in contrast to our sub-conscious mind, which is a vast reservoir of information with immense retrieval capacity. Whatever, we allow to get into our conscious mind, it gets stored in the subconscious mind. Whatever gets restored in the subconscious mind, this part of mind retrieves the relevant piece of information to help you take your next big or small decision. For example, if you always think about fear or scarcity or any other negative thoughts, they do the job of accumulation of junk information in your sub-conscious mind through your conscious brain.

But, in order to perform at best levels, our mind and body need to be energetic, focused, and distraction-free, so our mind can focus on our important work. Therefore, it becomes very important to safeguard our brain's cognitive powers and ensure that it doesn't get wasted on nondeserving thoughts or less-worthy pursuits. To maintain our cognitive abilities, we need to take few necessary precautions, so that we could use mental reservoirs to take actions towards our true desires.

a. Be Smart With Smartphone

The smartphone is probably the only one technological invention that almost stays with you more than your shadow. This smart device has such an addictive power, probably the severity of which is equivalent, if not more than smoking cigarettes or drinking. Smartphones consume a significant amount of our attention, willpower, and cognitive abilities.

You would agree that it is too difficult to resist the temptation to check your phone when it is near you. Such resistance to avoid looking at your phone itself will consume a lot of your mental energy. Instead of devoting your cognitive energy to what you are truly trying to accomplish, a good portion of it instead goes toward thinking about checking your phone, imagining what might be awaiting you on it, and simultaneously restraining yourself from actually checking it.

From a study published in *The Journal of Social Psychology*, researchers asked a group of college students to complete a series of difficult motor tasks when their cell phones were visible. Sure enough, their performance was significantly worse than a controlled group where participants' cell phones were not visible. Things got even more interesting when all the participants' cell phones were removed but the study leader's cell phone remained present. Surprisingly, even when the phone visible wasn't their own, the participants' performance suffered.

Why is that so?

There are evidences now that smartphone and the apps are designed in such a way that they do the job of making you addicted to these technologies. One of the renowned technology company's ex product manager did a candid revelation in an interview[6] stating that the objective of the technology and the online app companies is to hook the attention of the people. He compared the smartphone and the apps installed therein to a slot machine, wherein if someone starts looking, the machine hooks him by giving some instant reward in the form of new messages, likes or follows etc. The objective of the app is not primarily to give the advantage to people, rather to make them feel that the smartphone and the apps are indispensable. There is a psychology behind this known as ***theory of unexpected reward***. Every time you look at your smartphone, you would see get notification or news or alert. You are not even finished reading the one, immediately it is shown that there are new related stories that you may want to watch or listen. He compared this approach to

---

[6] https://vimeo.com/212594078

reaching and capturing the brainstem of humans. Because that's the way these for-profit companies would be able to grab attention and sell them the product and services later on.

Therefore, for any high-performance enthusiast, use of a smartphone has to be minimal, just need-based and once used immediately it should go away from the reach. I personally put my phone on airplane mode when I generally don't expect any phone calls for few hours. At times, I keep the phone on just to take phone calls; but deactivate the internet options. By this approach, I can focus better on my creative work i.e. writing books and other projects and enhance my performance. Once I am done with my quality work, then I put the phone on and check the notifications, alerts, etc., and generally I find I didn't miss anything major during those hours.

But I agree, everyone has his own circumstances or unique situation and the use of asmartphone can vary accordingly, but the basic idea is to use the smartphone to become *smarter*, and not become *addicted*. Depending upon your role and responsibility in your organization or if you work for your own, you should minimize the use of a smartphone as much as you can. This will help you to improve your performance.

b. Turn Off the TV:

Since the invention of television, it has become one of the primary means by which most people relax and recover. But, for the most part, however, watching television is the mental and emotional equivalent of eating junk food. You may feel a temporary form of recovery by watching television, but it is rarely nutritious, and it is easy to consume too much. Again, like smartphones, TV is another addiction tool to serve you commercials and advertisements that make you reach for your wallet to buy the advertiser's products.

Researchers, such as Mihaly Csikszentmihalyi, have found that prolonged television watching is actually correlated with increased anxiety and low-level depression.

There are better alternatives for doing recreation. Why not to go for a walk with your loved ones in the evening, instead of hitting the couch? Reading a great book, doing yoga or some meditation, playing with your kids are the healthy and nutritious food for your brain. These activities will help you feel more joyful, rather than watching a thriller or drama episodes, which will make you more exhausted after sitting for long hours.

To conclude, while it is very significant to make mental shifts for building your resilience to ensure better performance, but at the same time, you need to be mindful that our reservoirs don't simultaneously depleted by the excessive use of addictive technology. Please make sure that bucket of your brain doesn't have holes of addictions, so that it can amass and store good reserves of wisdom to use towards performing at your best levels.

With that now let's move on to the next section now, where you will learn how to master any skill by following the right principles.

Chapter 5: Proven Principles To Acquire Any New Skill Faster

****

"Acquire knowledge. Acquire skills. They weigh nothing, and you can carry them with you all your life."

~ Ruskin Bond"

Your drive to perform at your highest level would require you to continuously learn new skills. It is because always performing at the highest level means you need to evolve and unleash your true inner potential, which requires life-time learning of most effective ways to deliver the result faster.

Thankfully, we are now aware of proven concepts of homeostatis and neuroplasticity that almost assure you that you can reach any levels of growth if you truly desire, barring a few genetic limitations. Now you can ask your inner critic to shut up whining about your false limits that got imprinted on your mind due to social conditioning of past. You know very well now that our body is adaptable to anything and our mind is malleable and can be molded to change to any extent we want. These laws give you an understanding and assurance that you can become an altogether different person, which you had always wanted to become, regardless of location, religion, color, caste, gender, and you can reach to any heights, as you may desire.

Though it might sound repetitive, but I am intentionally choosing to do so. It is because, most people are wired to think their abilities and skill sets are limited or they are unable to learn something after a certain age. To break those myths and to rewire such mindsets, it becomes necessary to re-emphasize, because, as is rightly said below by this highly successful personality:

> *"Repetition is the mother of learning, the father of action, which makes it the architect of accomplishment."* ~ *Zig Ziglar* —

Therefore, these principles are worth engraving as a tattoo on your brain, as these are so important— to rewire your belief system about the limitlessness of human potential.

Okay, now with a deeper clarity on the above principles, we now move to the 'nuts and bolts' or 'How to' aspects. We will talk about a few strategies or techniques that will help you to learn new skills at a faster pace and without getting burned out. This section of the book is all about developing and mastering any skills.

Now let's look at these strategies:

1. The principle of stress and recovery:

When I go to my gym, I see a poster of Muhammad Ali with the inspiring quote:

> *'I don't count my sit-ups; I only start counting when it starts hurting because they're the only ones that count.'*

This would also remind you of famous saying: *"**No pain, no gain**"*.

You have to expose yourself to a level of stress in any area if you want to grow in that field. If you wish to build up your biceps or want to see yourself enjoying at beaches with your solid six-pack abdomen or if not that a fitter body even, you know that it takes work. It doesn't happen with only normal body movement. You have to stress the muscles which you want to grow.

This principle applies everywhere. If you want to acquire a mental skill or improve your thinking you have to stretch your mind beyond the normal.

Everyone knows. But this is half of the principle of gaining any physical muscle or mastering any skill. It is not that you would continuously stress or stretch yourself. The other half of the principle is *recovery*.

In sports and every other area of life, the principle of growth remains the same - a fair combination of stress and recovery periods. It means you first need to stress your body and then give yourself the requisite rest.

There the ultimate equation for growth without burn-out is:

Stress + Recovery= Growth

Jim Loehr, a performance psychologist in his book called *Toughness Training for Life* emphasizes on the above formula in below words:

> It's important to understand that only rarely does the volume of stress defeat us; far more often the agent of defeat is insufficient capacity for recovery after the stress. Great stress simply requires great recovery. Your goal in toughness, therefore, is to be able to spike powerful waves of

stress followed by equally powerful troughs of recovery. So here is an essential Toughness Training Principle: **Work hard. Recover equally hard.**

From a training perspective then, training recovery should receive as much attention as training stress. Unfortunately, that is rarely the case.

He puts it this way:

"Precisely the stress is the stimulus for growth. Recovery is when you grow."

How much stress and how much recovery?

The principle that needs to be kept in mind is to take just manageable challenges. There is a goldilocks principle to that —means something just right. Not too easy, but not too hard – it should be just manageable.

We should be stretching but not snapping. We are at the right edge where growth occurs without injury.

It should be a stress beyond your current capacity, but at the same time, you should not end up injuring yourself. If you get injured, that will demoralize you – moreover, if injured, you have no choice but to take a break which will kill the flow and rhythm of your training.

Let's take an example. Assuming you have never run long distances and now you want to give yourself a challenge of running a marathon. In almost all cases, it will make you nervous, if you think of the daunting task of running *twenty-six* miles all of a sudden, if you have no idea about the trainings or structure for planning such long runs.

I personally went through this phase – though it was not a full marathon, but a shorter distance race. I had been thinking for few years to participate in a half marathon. But it always seemed to me to be much beyond my capacity or stamina and too hard to handle. You would admit that simply being aware of the principles of adaptability don't help, howsoever hard you try to force something new and challenging upon you. You have to have some effective strategies to bring that change. The right strategy here is to take up the something challenging, but not way beyond your existing level of competency: it should be a challenge but something that you can manage to start with.

Let me share how I personally mastered the skill or running. The very first thing I did was to search on the internet about such trainings. I found few running training guides easily, thanks to Google. These guides told me to start effectively and gradually increase the stress level i.e. distance of running. Moreover, I learnt that once I start doing half a mile on the first day, I couldn't keep on increasing every day. The trainings told me that I have to first build my capacity and stamina for running a particular distance for few days – and then increase the distance by half a mile as a next step. Also, I was not supposed to run every day, rather I was required to do some other exercises on alternate days like cross fit or some aerobic exercise to stretch my whole body that could as well give rest to my legs and feet muscles. With that approach, I was able to run up to *six* kilometers in a period of *eight* weeks and in *twelve* weeks period, I was running up to *ten* kilometers. Then I participated in my first six kilometers race in one half marathon event.

I know it is not that big of an achievement, but I thought to honestly let you know about the principle of stress and recovery mechanism in place - though not knowing fully about the science behind that. You would notice that the principles of stress with levels thereof needed, and duration of recovery were tightly structured in the helpful training I went through for my race.

Is there magic number by which one should stretch?

To some people, following the goldilocks principle i.e. assessing what is 'something just right', may not give the precise idea or guidance. There was some research done by Steve Kotler the author of the book: *The Rise of Superman*, where he tells us about the magic stretch number being *four percent* beyond your existing capacity. He says

> "This is why the challenge/skills ratio is so important. If we want to achieve the kinds of accelerated performance we're seeing in action and adventure sports, then it's 4 percent plus 4 percent plus 4 percent, day after day, week after week, months into years into careers. This is the road to real

magic. Follow this path long enough, and not only does impossible becomes possible, it becomes what's next—like eating breakfast, like another day at the office."

To me *four percent* increase at a time seems just something right and not that hard. It is like, if you can do *twenty-five* pushups in a day, then, your stretch would be just one more push-up adding the next time you do it.

Finally, when the principle of manageable stretch fuses with the principle of compound effect the real magic starts then only. Daily small progress at incremental level would surprise you, if seen from a longer horizon of timeframe. In fact, you would look at you and your results and wonder what you have become and how far you had come with your consistent progress with manageable stretches.

As a writer, I know that if one consistently writes between 1,500-2,000 words in a day, then it will take him up to three weeks (with some rest days included) to see a first draft of manuscript of reasonably sized book. This many words per day is a stretch for anyone starting out, but it is still manageable- as compared to writing a book sitting at length in a stretch. It doesn't burn out and gives you a reasonable period to recover too.

Therefore, use the principles of Stress and recovery, because only that way it leads to the real growth. Because continuous stress and no recovery, you are leading to burnout. Very low stress or no stress, on the other hand would mean no growth at all. The right advice is to follow the goldilocks principle. Take the manageable challenges. Get the required rest after a period of stress and all this together on a consistent basis, will lead you to acquire any skills in a reasonably quantifiable period.

Can we introduce rest period even in high stake and stressful performance zone?

The concept of the stress and recovery not only applies in voluntary attempts to gain muscles or acquire new skills, i.e. a period when we are in low stake environment. But it is also very well introduced by high performers even when they are in high stake environment, when repercussions of any mistake are catastrophic.

It is of course difficult to fathom the idea of taking any long recovery break when you are in the midst of real action happening. You would rather argue that there is even no luxury or scope of taking smallest amount of rest or recovery, when you are in high stake performance zone.

You would give the example that in the midst of an argument in a high-stake litigation matter in court, a lawyer doesn't have the luxury of time to stop arguing the case, take rest, think about it and resume the argument after that. No, you don't see this happening this way ever.

But I have something surprising here to tell that even in the tough and highly demanding situations, when you can't imagine of taking any rest, high-performance develop the skill of stealing the briefest of recovery period (of few seconds) – and that changes the entire game. Let's look at a real-life example to support this point.

Jim Loehr And Tony Schwartz in their book *The Power of Full Engagement: Managing Energy, Not Time, is the Key to High Performance and Personal Renewal* give an example about how the best tennis players are able to maintain their level of performance till the last sets of the game, when they have exhausted substantial portion of their physical energy and stamina. You would simply give a rationale that they have developed the stamina to sustain for longer period of time by practice.

But the close observation of these extreme players revealed the **subtle infusion of the element of rest** even in the highly demanding and high-stake championship match of tennis. Jim Loehr states in his book that in his role as a performance psychologist, he had set a goal to understand the factors that set apart the greatest competitors in the world from the rest of the pack. He was working with world-class tennis players and had already spent hundreds of hours watching top players and studying tapes of their matches. To his growing frustration, he could detect almost no significant differences in their competitive habits during the game points.

It was only when he began to notice what these high-performers did between points that he suddenly saw a subtle difference. While most of them were not aware of it, the best players had each built almost exactly the same set of routines between points. These included the way they walked back to the baseline after a point; how they held their heads and shoulders; where they focused their eyes; the pattern of their breathing; and even the way they talked to themselves.

Authors explains that in those *sixteen to twenty* seconds between the points, the best tennis players were able to *lower their heart rates by as much as twenty beats per minute*. The heart rates of their competitors who didn't have the same dialed-in rest rituals often stayed at the same levels.

From the above, it becomes amply clear that one player who is able to squeeze in *twenty* seconds of rest after an intense game point, as compared to the another one who is just pushing himself hard and relying more on his stamina and willpower, will be in a better position to win the game. The player who grabbed mini recovery periods in those intense game points has already generated additional reservoir energy, while his competitor is consistently depleting his energy after each game point, will definitely overpower the latter.

Similarly, in the business world, when the financial or business stakes are high, when one has to make tough decisions and execute them, the key executives take deeper breaths, to get calmer; as their approach to create the recovery period and re-energize them to deliver their best performance.

2. Travel between Learning zone and performance zone.

We all know there is only one thing constant in life – that's called 'change'. While we might think that we have grown and can handle bigger task now, but that along with us the challenges of life and complexities do also add up. Our competitors in the pursuits we have chosen to also grow and learn the newer skills.

As you know high performance means to perform at your best levels and in a sustainable manner. If you have developed a particular skill, you are applying that already in your work or performance zone. But here is the thing. If you just stay in your performance zone with ab existing level of skill, the frequent changes in your work, or technology will soon make your current skill set as obsolete. Therefore, to enable you to play your game at your best- for long period – in a sustainable manner, you have to do something different.

Yes, you have to consistently travel between your performance zone and the learning zone. Learning zones means the time period in our lives, when we are focused on learning to improve our skills. On the other hand, performance zones are the areas when we are just performing the skills we learn.

The learning zone is when our goal is to improve. Then we do activities designed for improvement, concentrating on what we haven't mastered yet, which means we have to expect to make mistakes, knowing that we will learn from them. That is entirely different from what we do when we're in our performance zone. In the performance zone our goal is to do something as best as we can, to execute. In this zone, we concentrate on what we have already mastered, and we try to minimize mistakes.

One of the key requirements for high performance that most highly effective people follow is to continuously travel between the learning zone and the performance zone. They go through life deliberately alternating between two zones: the learning zone and the performance zone

You know, the problem with most of us is that we think that after we are out of school, college and earned our degrees or diplomas, the learning stops there -we think that now we have learnt, and it is the time to start performing.

In a wonderful talk by Eduardo Briceno, co-founder & CEO of Mindset Works, a growth mindset training company, he goes deeper into how we can get better at things we do care about. He gives the example of Demosthenes, a political leader, great orator in ancient Greece, and lawyer. In order to become a great orator and a good lawyer, he didn't always remain in the performance zone. Rather he spent time on learning the skills. He studied long hours about law and philosophy. But he also heard many great speeches to learn and master his public speaking skills. He had some lisp problem (a minor speech defect), so in order to speak clearly, he used to put stones in his mouth and then practice speaking. Such practice with greater emphasis on learning in the correct way and improve yourself by feedback is called deliberate practice (which I have covered in detail in the next chapter).

You would notice the people around the world, more they are successful; more they spend in learning zone. They simply don't remain in the performance zone. Look at the practice sessions of Olympic gold medalists, and other athletes – everyone spends an enormous amount of time in learning and practicing their craft. You will find CEOs and top notch corporate officials, spending significant times in conferences, learning from other industry colleagues. They clearly have understood that if they simply remain in the performance zone, they will just maintain the *status quo*. They know it is the learning zone that will help them to improve their knowledge and skills that will prepare them for next level of growth and enhance their competence to perform better.

I had been a corporate lawyer for many years and can confirm one thing based on my interaction with many legal eagles. They travel between the learning zone and the performance zone almost every day. More particularly, a litigation lawyer argues cases in court all day long, and then in the evening and for long nights sometimes, he researches the court's orders and case laws related to the litigation matters, which are lined upthe next morning. The same is true with other professions like accountants, doctors, or engineers.

This is because these high performers know that staying in the performance zone keeps their performance at their current level. But getting into the learning zone helps you to improve your future and achieve more in life.

Eduardo gives another example of Beyoncé, an American singer and songwriter, who also consistently travels between learning zone and the performance zone. When she is performing a show in the evening, she is in the performance zone. But once her show is over, she then enters the learning zone. She is known to watch the videos of her shows in the evening and note the areas that could be improved for the next day. On the next morning, her team of musicians, dancers, and other staff get pages of notes on what needs to be tweaked in the next show. Therefore, she is on the continuous journey between the leaning zone and the performance zone.

With all that, the next question that comes up is: how can we spend more time in the learning zone? There are few ways to do that as Eduardo suggests the first and foremost condition is that we must believe that we can improve. That's what is referred to as growth mindset by researcher Carol Dweck. Secondly, we all must have a desire to learn, as nothing moves until we truly desire to improve. Next, we need to create some low stake environments, where even if we do something wrong, there should not be any catastrophic outcomes. For example, a tightrope walker doesn't practice new tricks without a net underneath them, and an athlete wouldn't set out to first try a new move during a championship match.

Because our environments are always too high stakes, so we have no choice except to remain in our performance zones. Most of the corporate cultures these days promote flawless execution, and that's good approach. But beneath this culture there should be some scope of trying newer ways, experimenting innovative ideas knowing that the idea may go wrong. But trying and testing different ways is also the way to learn and improve in anything. But what should be the approach for switching to learning zone, in such high-stake performance zone? The solution is to create low stake islands in the high stake sees. It is by way of talking to our mentors or trusted colleagues with who we can talk about the things we don't know, or we need to improve upon. People should be given some time to learn newer techniques through education conferences or by way of attending seminars or conferences.

If someone can work towards shifting the gears between the learning zone and the performance zone, that is almost a sure-shot way to high performance. That's why it is said practice doesn't make a man perfect. It is the right practice that makes a man practice. If you get into the real world of action after learning the better ways to perform, people will realize the qualitative improvement in your performance- and that way you will set yourself apart from the crowd.

The next section of the book will build upon what you learnt in the current section. It will teach you the best way to learn by a refined form of practice that is necessary to gain mastery and expertise in any skill.

With that, let's jump to the next section of this book.

Chapter 6: The Science of Expertise – How Highly Successful Attain Mastery

****

"Mastery is not a function of genius or talent. It is a function of time and intense focus applied to a particular field of knowledge."

~ Robert Greene

Everyone has heard the age old saying:

"Practice makes a man perfect."

But sadly, this is not entirely true.

You might think that the more experience you have doing something, the better you get. But that's not true. You don't become better driver by driving more or for a longer period. You don't become a better doctor by just being a doctor for several years. You don't become a better accountant or a lawyer just by being that. It is like someone claiming *twenty* years of experience in a field, but in reality it could be one year of experience just repeated over *twenty* years without learning anything new in that time.

Therefore, practicing the same things over and over without focus on improving your craft doesn't make you any better — forget becoming perfect. Hence, the improved version of this quote should be:

"Perfect practice makes a man perfect".

You get better not merely by practicing something, but by practicing it the right way. This section is about teaching what should be the right way to practice. Anders Ericsson, is a psychologist and researcher at Florida State University, he was the original researcher on the famous 10,000-hour rule, which was promoted Malcolm

Gladwell in his famous book *Outliers,* as the necessary time period needed to become an expert in any filed.

Ericsson explains that there are three types of practices, which people pursue to gain any skill in any field, as stated below:

a. Naive Practice
b. Purposeful Practice
c. Deliberate Practice.

Let's look at each of these one by one and learn why Ericsson emphasizes that only deliberate practice is the way to attaining the status of expert or master of any particular field.

1. **Naive practice** means a generic kind of mindless practice, where you simply keep on doing what you had learnt earlier. It's like always being in the performance zone and just taking actions only based on your existing knowledge and skill set without any focus or intention of improvement. This type of practice

of doing the same thing repeatedly and expecting that it will improve, does not work at all. Rather, this was termed as insanity by the famous Albert Einstein:

> *"The definition of insanity is doing the same thing over and over and expecting different results."*

It is like playing guitar from your college days till your *forties*, without deliberately learning the best ways to press the right nodes and strings — and expecting that the *twenty* years of practice will make you a better guitarist. You don't get the exact benefit of the feature of adaptability of human body and mind by repeating the same thing mindlessly over and over again.

Then what makes the difference? For this let's first look at other two types of practices.

2. **Purposeful Practice**: This is a better way to practice and learn a skill faster, as compared to naive practice, but still a level below the deliberate practice. Here are the features of a purposeful practice:

   a. Purposeful practice has <u>well-defined and specified goals</u>. Take the example of any sports training or learning any new language or playing any musical instrument within a particular time frame. Here you have a clear objective to learn a skill in a particular time frame.

   b. Purposeful practice is <u>focused</u>

This kind of practice is not like planning a casual trip to your grocery store to wander around and grab something. No, it doesn't work that way. Purposeful practice is not something that is fun or relaxing work. Rather it is to be entirely focused on that activity. If you are allowing anything and everything to disturb you in that activity, that's not a focused practice – you will end up wasting your time – and forget about learning anything.

c. Purposeful practice <u>requires feedback</u>

You need to know how you're doing step by step. Did you miss a note playing that song you want to play perfectly four times in today's practice? <u>Immediate feedback to help you identify what you're doing wrong</u> (and how you can improve) is essential.

d. Purposeful practice wants you to <u>get out of your comfort zone</u>

This is one of the most important elements of purposeful practice. If you don't push yourself beyond your comfort zone, you will never improve.

Anyone can realize that practicing with well-defined and specific goals, in a focused manner, with an appropriate feedback system about your mistakes, and with consistent pushing beyond the comfort zone – contains all the necessary triggers to improve learning and performance. That's why purposeful practice is certainly a great way to learn anything new. But there is something more that works wonders when it comes to practicing and seeking high performance, and that's called deliberate practice:

3. **Deliberate Practice:** That's called a gold standard of any practice. This practice has all the elements of the purposeful practice, but it additionally has the element of coaching or teaching added to it, through a clear training program in the established field.

Deliberate practice involves the pursuit of personal improvement via well-defined, specific goals and targeted areas of expertise, as required in purposeful practice, but additionally, it requires a teacher or coach who has demonstrated an ability to help others improve the desired area of expertise—say chess, tennis, or music—and who can give continuous feedback.

Think about Tiger Woods, the titan of the golf. Do you think he needs any training or coaching for golf? He hired a swing coach for long period of times to correct his swing. He knew very well an expensive club set wouldn't make him win the game - it was the mastery of his craft that would keep him at the apex position. He knows the importance of deliberate practice under expert guidance to consistently improve and master his game.

Ericsson states that just working harder or working more does not seem to be associated with high levels of performance.

Rather, if you're working with a teacher or a mentor who has attained this high level of performance, that individual can help you now design the kind of training activities that they may have engaged in order to reach that higher level of performance.

He states: "It's not just a matter of accumulating hours. If you're doing your job, and you're just doing more and more of the same, you're not actually going to get better."

It will be useful here to cite[7] an illustration of normal practice versus deliberate practice to understand it better.

Normal Practice

- Start with a general idea of what the kid wants to do (play tennis)
- Find a tennis group or lessons, play with parents, siblings, friends

---

[7] https://qz.com/915646/how-to-make-your-kid-good-at-anything-according-to-anders-ericsson-an-expert-on-peak-performance-and-originator-of-the-10000-hour-rule/

- Practice until kid reaches an acceptable level
- Get a coach
- Play more
- Continue improving.

Deliberate practice

- Start with a general idea of what the kid wants to do (play tennis)
- Find a tennis group or lessons, play with parents, siblings, friends
- Practice until kid reaches an acceptable level
- Get a coach who can set specific targets and tailor practice to improve those areas (improve forehand)
- Develop a way to measure improvement, so if forehands are a weakness, the coach delivers lots of those strokes, progressively makes them harder to return, and demands that the player places strokes in a specific spot. Progress is tracked constantly.

- Create positive channels for feedback so that modifications are continuous (like learning how not to reveal intentions to opponent).
- Develop a mental representation of excellent performance: what to do in various game situations; how to respond to certain shots; when to take risks and try new things.
- A coach designs developmentally appropriate training sessions to achieve maximum effort and concentration.
- A kid learns to self-assess and come up with own mental representations, so they feel in charge and able to exploit opportunities on the court
- A kid develops own training sessions to elicit maximum effort and concentration, acknowledging physical and mental limits, and learns to use self-assessment to address weaknesses.

You can now easily understand why experts appear to be so effortless, because the underlying deliberate practice has already made strong mental representations in their head that helps them to take quick decisions in real-time. Ericsson succinctly explains how the inner brain structure and neural circuit changes with deliberate practice in below words:

> The main thing that sets experts apart from the rest of us is that their years of practice have changed the neural circuitry in their brains to produce highly specialized mental representations, which in turn make possible the incredible memory, pattern recognition, problem-solving, and other sorts of advanced abilities needed to excel in their particular specialties. The more you study a subject, the more detailed your mental representations of it become, and the better you get at assimilating new information.

I loved his wonderful thoughts where he says:

"There is no reason not to follow your dream. Deliberate practice can open the door to a world of possibilities that you may have been convinced were out of reach. Open that door."

The above statement is definitely an assurance to reach for and achieve anything you want to achieve in your life and the tools of deliberate practice will make it possible for you to fulfill your dreams.

Chapter 7: Key Tenets to Activate High Performance in Your Everyday Life

****

"Successful people do what unsuccessful people are not willing to do." ~ Jeff Olson

A good life is nothing but a combination of intentionally well lived days in a row for longer periods of time. If we take care of our days, we don't need to worry about our future and it will make our past beautiful. A well planned and well lived day will build on the strong foundation for a better tomorrow – and when you look back at such days in a row- you will feel great about your past too.

Robin Sharma once rightly said: *"Small daily improvements over time lead to stunning results."*

Since, we are on this journey to perform at our highest level, so the first requirement is to become intentional to plan our days and imbibe the self-discipline to overcome our inner resistances. You need to keep your cravings for instant gratification at bay and focus on the activities that will make your closer to your goals. This section explains few strategies that will help you take charge of your everyday actions. Let's look at these strategies now:

1. Apply W.I.N. Formula to Control Your Moment to Moment Decisions:

What is this W.I.N. Formula?

This is the strategy that highly successful use to take their moment to moment decisions, that enables them to craft their best days – and thus achieve results.

W.I.N. stands for **What's Important Now**. This acronym was used by Bob Bowman, coach to the legend Michael Phelps, an American swimmer and one of the most prized Olympic athletes in the History.

In his book, *No Limits-The Will To Succeed* Michael Phelps explains the secrets behind all his legendary performances and winning of Olympic medals, including his coach's Bob Bowman strategies. There is a mention in the book, where coach Bob Bowman explains what separates Michael from all other swimmers. Bowman states that if other swimmers don't feel good, they don't swim good. But this was not the case with Michael. He performs regardless of what he feels, as he has trained his mind with his practice for a long period.

Michael shows that high performers don't let their feelings come in the way of their actions. If something is to be done as a priority, then they perform at their best, despite whatever they feel about that activity. Their feelings are not important, rather the action towards the goal is important.

Anyone can conclude that if you have strong self-control and can control your emotions effectively, then no one can stop you from taking action towards your goals. It wouldn't be incorrect to say that on most occasions it is rather our inner critic mind that interrupts in our performance, and not the outside circumstances.

Michal's criterion for making a decision at any given moment is simple **"What's Important Now"** and not "*How do I feel now*". Ultimately, it is this W.I.N. formula that triggers him to take massive action towards his goals, and with strong self-discipline on his feelings, he is able to master his game.

Just feel yourself the conviction, in the words of Michael Phelps, when he says:

"*It's true. When it comes down to it, when the time comes to focus and be mentally prepared, I can do whatever it takes to get there, in any situation.*"

There is no ambiguity, no second thought in his mind – it's just a solid decision. Life becomes quite easy when you master such kind of self-discipline in your life.

On the similar lines of W.I.N. Formula, Eric Greitens, a former Navy SEAL officer, writes in his book *Resilience: Hard-Won Wisdom for Living a Better Life,* explains that your actions should be based on what you want to become, i.e. your future identity. It's never a right approach to take action on the basis of what you feel.

Simply put, your actions should be driven by the identity that you want to achieve and not by what you feel about the activity at any given point of time. The factor of feeling comes at the last in this formula. It goes like this:

Identity > Action > Feelings

Whenever you have a dilemma about taking action, ask yourself, *'Who I want to become?'* And the answer to that question will guide you to take the right action –and that action will lead you closer to what you want to become. With that sense of clarity about your direction, the level of energy you will put to your work will be entirely different (in a positive way), as compared to actions taken based on what you feel. You will perform with greater determination and a sense of urgency towards your goal with this approach.

And the best part is that once you can take massive actions, you will move forward- you will either see results or get some lessons, and that way will make you feel better.

In the above equation, you would realize that instead of making your feelings the dominant factor to take actions, you have simply put it at the end of the equation. There, the whole sequence is reversed for your benefit. Now, your feelings are just an outcome of the quality of actions taken by you.

Don't go by your feelings to decide your next action step – they will simply leave you in the lurch. If you are in a good mood one day, you work your butt off; but next day, if you don't feel better, you just spoil your day. There are already so many uncontrollable outside factors that you need to overcome on your journey towards your goal, and additionally your negative feelings to it are going to make your life much harder.

Taking the case of Michael Phelps – he knew what he wanted to become – the best in the world in his game. Thus, the W.I.N. principle guided him to take the right action for him to attain that identity of a world-class swimmer. The actions taken on the right underlying factors lead to performance at a heightened level, which delivers the best results. So finally – goal achieved and you FEEL superb now. And that's the way to go.

What kind of action leads to high performance?

Okay, let's take it one step further.

So far, based on the identity that you have chosen for yourself, you apply the W.I.N. formula to take the immediate action that's most important for you. Since, we are talking about achieving the state of high performance; it is quite relevant here to talk about the level and quality of actions to be taken more specifically. Grant Cardone in his book *The 10X Rule: The Only Difference Between Success and Failure* squarely addresses this point in below words:

"One question I've received over the years is, 'Exactly how *much* action is necessary to create success?' Not surprisingly, everyone is looking for the secret shortcut—and equally unsurprising is the following fact: There are no shortcuts. <u>The more action you take, the better your chances are of getting a break</u>. Disciplined, consistent, and persistent actions are more of a

117

determining factor in the creation of success than any other combination of things. Understanding how to calculate and then take the right amount of action is more important than your concept, idea, invention, or business plan"

Grant further states that most people fail because they are operating at the wrong degree of action. He goes on to categorize the actions based the degree of involvement as below. For taking any action, one can have these four choices:

1. Do nothing.

2. Retreat.

3. Take normal levels of action.

4. Take massive action.

You have to take massive action to attain the state of high performance and just look at the reason why Grant emphasis the power of massive action, when he says:

'Overcommit, be all in, and take massive levels of action followed up by massive amounts of more actions. You will create new problems and deliver at levels that will amaze even you."

Be clear in your mind that any lukewarm actions do not work- they will give you only lukewarm results. If you keep on doubting yourself and take action in that state, you can create the required high momentum in your actions. In fact, you are trying to deceive yourself here. Your mind will try to convince you that you are taking action, but at the same time, you will find yourself doubting and slowing down your actions. This approach doesn't work.

Therefore, massive action in the direction of your destiny is the only way to go.

Now let's talk about the next strategy to incorporate high performance in your days:

2. **Set Product Goal & Process goals.**

> *"Set Product Goals and Emphasize Process Goals: To achieve greatness, you must set end goals and place significant emphasis on what it takes to accomplish them."*
>
> *~ Jason Selk*

We all know about goal setting. We know that we should be setting SMART goals, i.e. they should be Specific, Measurable, Attainable, Relevant, and Time-bound. But the key thing about these goals is they are always appearing us to be obtained in future. Sometimes that very reason becomes a hindrance to achieve those goals. We keep on thinking that we always have time to achieve that goal. That's why most people set almost the same goals every year.

The solution lies in setting two categories of goals:

1. Product goals
2. Process goals.

Jason Selk, one of the world's leading peak performance coaches uses this terminology of product goal and process goals in one of his book. Let's understand this better and how this lead to achieving your goal of high performance.

Product goals are the goals that are <u>result oriented</u> and are potentially attainable with a period of next 12 months. For example, if you have a goal of running a half-marathon in next six month or a full marathon in twelve months, that will be your product goal. Product goals are specific in terms of results and the timelines to attain those goals.

Process goals are goals that are <u>action oriented</u> – they focus on what actions are needed to be taken on a daily basis to achieve your product goals. This is important to set the process goal for every product goal. Because it is very easy to set up a goal that is far away six months or one year, but when we see the goal still a few months away, we tend to drift assuming that we have enough time to achieve those. We think that we will be able to catch up sooner on those goals when we reach closer to the deadline. But it doesn't work that way usually – because if we start drifting that becomes a vicious circle. Skipping one day leads to skipping another day and soon you would realize that you have not worked for days, weeks, or even months giving one excuse or the other. Here process goals come to your rescue.

Jason recommends that we should have two or three process goals for each of the product goals. Sometimes a process goal may happen less frequently than every day, but it still needs to occur on a regular basis to drive the achievement of the product goal. Take your previous example of running a half marathon in six months from now, as your product goal, what should be your process goal? Here you need to have two to three process goals, and those could be as below:

a. Your daily running and exercise schedule to be followed without fail including the provisions for recovery days.
b. You have to daily ensure consumption of healthy diet and nutrients and avoid junk food.
c. You need to regularly go through your training guide or online course or consult your fitness coach, if you have engaged one, to ensure that you

are following the training correctly to avoid any injuries

The process goals are the immediate triggers that put you in action on a daily basis to make your closer to the distant product goal. Setting up product goals and process goals together not only gives a sense of direction but also ensures that you are on the track and achieving regular progress.

To put it differently, while the product goals show you the ultimate flag at the summit of the mountain, the process goals asks you to work on the goal every day and also have a sense of motivation if you covered the required distance in a particular day. Process goals also help you to avoid getting de-motivated because of the goals appearing so far in future, because you know that daily progress will ultimately lead to your product goals.

As is rightly said, ***"Well begun is half done".***

You need to start taking action based on the right parameters and keep on building momentum to achieve the level of high performance.

The summary of what we discussed in this section is below as a step plan to help you start taking action now:

- First and foremost, ask yourself what you want to become. Seek that answer deeply from within. How do you feel about that identity? Does it excite you? Does it feel like liberating if you'd achieved that identity? Does it feel like a 'resounding yes' or are you feel like dabbling between two choices? Remember Identity precedes activity. Until you claim your identity, you will not be motivated to take any action.

- Once you have got a convincing answer to who you are going to become, then don't let any temporary feelings of sadness, anxiety, fear of failure, fear of rejection, fear of missing out something overpower your mind. You have to simply take action that is most important to achieve the identity you have claimed. For example, before writing any book, I need to reclaim my identity as a writer. This immediately raises the next questions i.e. what should a writer do? And the obvious answer comes: write, write and write - what else? With that straightforward answer, I am in fact implementing the W.I.N. formula. Don't pay attention to any adverse feeling of doubts, anxiety, and worry and simply take action.

- To re-emphasize, your actions need to be massive and also on a regular basis. If you strongly believe in the identity you have chosen for you, you will find it easier to take action. Only massive actions taken on a consistent basis, almost on a daily basis give you instant feedback - that will help you to do the necessary course correction, if needed and move faster towards your goals. Below is what the importance of taking massive actions in the words of Grant Cardone, from *The 10x Rule:*

"The 10X Rule requires that you take action in massive quantities and immediately. Anyone who puts off doing what he or she can do right now will never gain the momentum and confidence that result from doing so."

Chapter 8: Scientific Ways to Boost Your Willpower for Sustained Performance

****

"Willpower and desire when properly combined make an irresistible pair"

~ Napoleon Hill

Willpower is one of the key elements that ensure that you achieve the state of high performance. We learnt in the previous sections that it is only the deliberate practice that leads to mastery, and also one needs to put massive action into the pursuit regardless of what one feels about it. You would agree that deliberate practice towards learning and putting consistent and massive actions requires you to control your urges to check your next social media notification, not getting swayed away easily by some outside distraction or other people around you. In short, the deliberate practice and consistent and massive actions that lead you to perform at your best – which requires willpower.

Roy Baumeister, a psychologist at Florida State University, describes[8] three necessary components for achieving your goals. First, you need to establish the motivation for change and set a clear goal. Second, you need to monitor your behavior toward that goal. The third component is willpower. Whether your goal is to lose weight, kick a smoking habit, study more, or spend less time on Facebook, willpower is a critical step to achieving that outcome.

Let's start with a simple definition of what is willpower.

---

[8] http://www.apa.org/helpcenter/willpower.aspx

Willpower is our ability to control and resist our short-term temptations to enable us to achieve our longer-term goals. It is also known as determination, self-control, drive or self-discipline. In terms of psychology, as many researchers in the field have defined it, willpower can be stated as:

- the ability to delay gratification, resisting short-term temptations to meet long-term goals.
- The capacity to override an unwanted thought, feeling, or impulse.
- The ability to employ a "cool" cognitive system of behavior rather than a "hot" emotional system.
- Conscious, effortful regulation of the self by the self.

With above definition, it is now evident that willpower is the force that can keep us glued to the actions that are important to achieve our long-term goals. As goals take a long time, our internal desires to enjoy instant gratification, often drift us from our path, and that's where willpower help us keep doing and delivering the highest level of performance.

In this section, we will talk about how one can develop willpower that enables one to take massive actions towards the goals. Let's look at some the best ways to improve your willpower:

1. Meditation significantly improves willpower

Whether it is East or West, you would agree that nowadays meditation is not something that one considers only as a religious or spiritual activity, rather it is benefits for the general well-being and improved functionality are well recognized by neuroscience already. It is not any mystical ritual – rather it has become a part of daily routine of many high-achievers, who start their day with some kind of mindfulness practice. Tim Ferriss, a best-selling author, who has also interviewed more than *two hundred* high achievers in the field of sports, business, entertainment confirms that more than *ninety percent* of these high-achiever interviewees have instilled the daily habit of some kind of meditation even if it is for few minutes a day

If you are new to this seemingly mystical word, meditation, let's briefly understand about meditation.

Meditation is nothing but a process of traveling inside your body and mind and enhancing your awareness about the ongoing thoughts, and emotions. One of the most common techniques to do meditation is to sit silently with your spine erect and focus on your breath only as anchor to observe regularly. This practice slowly enhances your consciousness and calms your mind, even if you do it daily for say ten minutes only. For beginning, you can do it with some guided meditation available through many free smartphone apps like Headspace, Calm, Welzen etc. In my book <u>*The Mindful Mind*</u>, I have captured various aspects of mindfulness, including the benefits as confirmed by neuroscience and the best ways to get started immediately.

I'd agree that for sitting in meditation on its own requires willpower, but it has immense benefits to develop your willpower.

In her book, *The Willpower Instinct: How Self-Control Works, Why It Matters, and What You Can Do To Get More of It,* the author Kelly Mcgonigal, psychologist and researcher describes the benefits of meditation on the willpower.

> Neuroscientists have now found that when we make ourselves sit and instruct our brain to meditate, not only it gets better at meditating, but it develops a wide range of self-control skills, including attention, focus, stress management, impulse control, and self-awareness. Science tells that people who meditate regularly for longer periods, have more gray matter in the prefrontal

cortex, as well as other regions of the brain that support self-awareness.

She further explains that you don't need a lifetime of meditation to see the results and explains intense meditation for few hours shows great results. She states:

Some researchers have started to look for the smallest dose of meditation needed to see benefits.... One study found that just three hours of meditation practice led to improved attention and self-control. After eleven hours, researchers could see those changes in the brain. The new meditators had increased neural connections between regions of the brain important for staying focused, ignoring distractions, and controlling impulses. Another study found that eight weeks of daily meditation practice led to increased self-awareness in everyday life, as well as increased gray matter in corresponding areas of the brain. It may seem incredible that our brains can reshape themselves so quickly, <u>but meditation increases blood flow to the prefrontal cortex, in much the same way that lifting weights increases blood flow to your muscles.</u> The brain appears to adapt to exercise in the same way that muscles do, getting both bigger and faster in order to get better at what you ask of it.

I've been meditating for quite few years now, but not very regularly. But over the last few months, I am doing it every morning and in the evening before going to bed. My personal experience is that I am starting to sense thoughts, emotions, and even tiny vibrations in my body. I am starting to make a fine distinction between different thoughts and emotions in my mind and body. The most important benefit is that I often find myself literally able to tell my negative emotions or the desires for instant gratification to get away from my mind—and simultaneously I can ask my mind to focus on resourceful thoughts that will lead me towards my goals. I can honestly tell you that it is an amazing feeling, when you can control yourself about what you should do next. I know it is a long journey, but if you keep moving, you will become closer day by day. One last thing, once you start meditating and start enjoying the benefits of it, then you won't feel like skipping it even for a single day.

Slow down your breath to beat stress:

As you just noted above that focusing on breathing is one of the common technique for meditation. But you would be surprised to know how one simple technique of slowing down your breathing pace helps to improve your willpower. This is what you need to do. Breathe slowly— so slow that it is just four to six breaths per minute only. Each breath in and out will take ten to fifteen second. It will be initially little difficult, but you can master it with some practice and it is not that hard.

Explaining the benefit of this technique of slow breathing, Kelly McGonigal states that the <u>slowdown of breathing activates the prefrontal cortex and increases heart rate variability, which helps shift the brain and body from a state of stress to self-control mode.</u> A few minutes of this technique will make you feel calm, in control, and capable of handling cravings or challenges

Therefore, breathe in for a count of four, and then breathe out for a count of six. Do it few times, and you will start getting the benefits of relieved from any anxiety but geared up for taking the next action.

Remember, you don't need to hold the breath. It will rather increase the stress. One another important thing that I have learnt in my meditation practices is that you should focus more on exhaling, rather than inhaling of your breathing. Once you pay attention more on emptying your body and leave no particle of any air in your body, it automatically takes care of breathing in.

Okay coming to next technique for developing willpower. Here it is:

2. Exercise is the wonder drug for willpower

We all know the famous quote from Albert Einstein:

"Nothing happens until something moves"

That applies to our bodies too. We have to move our bodies to bring our internal organs in good health by increasing blood circulation that gives us energy for performing at our best levels. Again, Psychologist Kelly McGonigal describes benefits of exercise as a wonder drug to develop your willpower. Here is what she states:

> Exercise turns out to be the closest thing to a wonder drug that self-control scientists have discovered. For starters, the willpower benefits of exercise are immediate. Fifteen minutes on a treadmill reduces cravings, as seen

when researchers try to tempt dieters with chocolate and smokers with cigarettes. The long-term effects of exercise are even more impressive. <u>It not only relieves ordinary, everyday stress, but it's as powerful an antidepressant as Prozac.</u> Working out also enhances the biology of self-control by increasing baseline heart rate variability and training the brain. When neuroscientists have peered inside the brains of new exercisers, they have seen <u>increases in both gray matter—brain cells—and white matter, the insulation on brain cells that help them communicate quickly and efficiently with each other</u>. Physical exercise—like meditation—makes your brain bigger and faster, and the prefrontal cortex shows the largest training effect.

You would have already realized that with specific tools and techniques like meditation, and exercise, it is not that hard to strengthen your willpower muscles. This enhanced willpower will help you to stay longer and perform better in your pursuits.

3. Use Self Control Exercises to Build Your willpower

Willpower is also like a muscle and if you get yourself committed to small self-control exercises on a regular basis, it will help you to build your willpower muscles. Seemingly insignificant activities like making your bed in the morning after you wake up; improving your sitting posture continuously, cutting back on sweets etc., play a role in improving your overall willpower.

Martha Beck, a sociologist life coach and author once said, "*The way we do anything is the way we do everything.*" If you practice exercising self-control on small and inconsequential things, you will tend to improve your willpower in important areas of your life i.e. focusing at your work, taking care of your health and tame your emotions better.

How small self-control exercises help us to develop our willpower is explained by Heidi Grant Halvorson in her book *Succeed*. She states:

> If you want more self-control, you can get more. And you get more self-control the same way you get bigger muscles—you've got to give it regular workouts. Recent research has shown that engaging in daily activities such as exercising, keeping track of your finances or what you are eating—or even just remembering to sit up straight every time you think of it—can help you develop your overall self-control capacity. For example, in one study, students who were assigned to (and stuck to) a daily exercise program not only got physically healthier, but they also became more likely to wash dishes instead of leaving them in the

sink, and less likely to impulsively spend money.

Developing willpower is one of the most important requirements if you want to bring significant changes in your life and perform at your best levels. One annual survey conducted by the American Psychological Association[9] about level of stress in America asks, among other things, about participants' abilities to make healthy lifestyle changes. Survey participants regularly cite lack of willpower as the #1 reason for not following through with such changes.

Fortunately, you don't need to spend hefty amount, take any medication, or visit any medical specialists to address your lack of willpower. The solutions are easily available to anyone at home. It is only a matter of putting in a very little sum of willpower to start with the techniques stated above, and anyone can start seeing the results in terms

---

[9] http://www.apa.org/helpcenter/willpower.aspx

of enhanced willpower. Of course, this will get you focused on your work longer and improve your performance.

4. Be Precise and Specific- Supports and Strengthens Willpower

Willpower depletes by vague directions. The more specific you are about the timing, and action to be taken, the more you will be able to use willpower to your advantage.

A few studies already confirm that specificity of timing and precision of behavior significantly increases the likelihood of success. This is because we have a limited amount of willpower during the day and every small decision depletes the willpower. Knowing this principle, many successful people pre-decide their routine things, so it doesn't take their willpower and time to decide. For example, they decide what clothes they will wear on each day of the week, is a decision they take every Sunday evening – for the entire next week. What food they are going to eat during the day – is already pre-decided.

Developing these routines is the key. You also need to remove the day-to-day problems that absorb most people for meaningful parts of their day. Former United States President Barack Obama once said, "You'll see I wear only gray or blue suits I'm trying to pare down decisions. <u>I don't want to make decisions about what I'm eating or wearing. Because I have too many other decisions to make.</u>" If we spend energy making too many little decisions, we'll have less to make the more important decisions.

Our pre-frontal cortex is responsible for executive decision making and other important functions that require conscious thinking efforts. By determining when, where and how any behavior will occur, we no longer have to think much about getting it done.

In one of the interesting experiments, a group of drug addicts were studied during withdrawal—a period of abrupt discontinuation or decrease in the intake of medications or recreational drugs. During this period, the energy required to control the urge to consume drug severely affects their ability to carry out any other task.

In this withdrawal period, one group of addicts was asked to commit to writing a short resume before a particular time on a particular day. This was to help them find post-rehabilitation employment. Not even one succeeded. A second group was asked to complete the same task, but the group was additionally told exactly when and where they would write the resume. The result was eighty percent of people in the second group succeed.

Therefore, specificity of time and precision of action to be taken safeguards the use of willpower. Next time, don't give yourself any vague instructions, rather you should tell yourself the precise time and precise action to avoid unnecessary wastage of your willpower, which is a precious resource.

Let's move to the next technique to enhance your willpower.

5. Rituals safeguard willpower:

All highly effective people use well-crafted rituals to perform their task. Rituals can be defined as carefully defined and well-structured behavior that are purposefully induced to our days.

As opposed to use of willpower and self-discipline, which requires pushing yourself to do a particular action, the rituals rather pull you towards them. Taking a shower in the morning, brushing your teeth are the daily rituals. You don't need to use any willpower or discipline yourself to undertake these morning routines –you never feel a need to push yourself to do these activities. You would have noticed in the previous point about how successful people safeguard their willpower by organizing their routine. Rituals ensure that we use as little conscious energy as possible where it is not absolutely necessary, leaving us free to strategically focus the energy available to us in more creative and productive ways.

All high performers rely on positive rituals to manage their energy and regulate their behavior. It is also said that more exciting the challenge and the greater the pressure, the more rigorous our rituals need to be. Robin Sharma, in his study of the world's high performers discovered one key thing – Consistency on the fundamentals. High performers don't need to think about fundamentals, as they have become their rituals.

Similarly, Jack Canfield, in his great book *The Success Principles* says that *"99% is a bitch and 100% is a breeze."*

If you have to use willpower or have to think about going to the gym every morning, that's not going to work, if you want to perform at your best levels. But once you commit and make going to gym as a ritual, then it happens almost on autopilot basis. You have to become non-negotiable in planning and adhering to your rituals. Only then it works.

With rituals formed for most of their daily activities, high performers benefitted in multiple ways:

- They can do most of the activities without even thinking about them, hence they can do more less time.

- They free up their mental space that can be used for highly creative and chaotic activities, which don't have a blueprint already and thus require most of your willpower and cognitive abilities.

- As they use the willpower for the most creative pursuits and finding solutions to the higher level of problems, they develop a greater sense of confidence, which in turns leads them to perform at much better pace in their pursuits.

Don't take your precious resource of willpower for granted. Safeguard this priceless gem for your high value activities with the support of well-crafted rituals- and very soon, you will find yourself in the category of ultra-performers.

Chapter 9: The Neuroscience of Peak Performance or 'Flow' State & How You Can Experience It.

****

"The happiest people spend much time in a state of flow - the state in which people are so involved in an activity that nothing else seems to matter; the experience itself is so enjoyable that people will do it even at great cost, for the sheer sake of doing it."

~ Mihaly Csikszentmihalyi

You must have heard about other people and probably you yourself might have had an experienced a state of mind when you are in a flow – that generally happens when you are engaged in something you are passionate about. Different names are given to this state of consciousness like 'runner's high', 'being in the zone' or 'peak performance'.

To define, 'flow' is the term used by researchers to indicate the optimal state of consciousness, those highest moments of total absorption by the activity we are into, in such a way that we lose our own sense of existence. In such states, time seems to fly and the performance of such person goes through the roof. The flow state has been described by the world's greatest thinkers as the most productive and creative state of mind in which work doesn't remain work anymore, rather it becomes a joy.

I see this as a state where there remains no difference between the doer and doing. For instance, if a dancer is in the state of flow while dancing, she forgets any difference between herself and dance. The dancer becomes the dance. It is a situation of complete immersion in the activity, where your entire focus is on the activity and you become insulated from any kind of distract (you will know the scientific rationale about this in a bit).

The above experiences might seem mystical or philosophical to few people. And flow obviously doesn't sound to be a sober scientific topic to be explored. Still there had been few people who were curious to explore about this concept of flow – to understand the science behind this and how does it feel, when someone experienced that state of being.

An Hungarian psychologist Mihaly Csikszentmihalyi was one such person who embarked upon this journey to dig deeper into this state of being that generates the highest levels of performance by an individual. He recognized and named this psychological concept for this heightened state of consciousness as "flow".

Csikszentmihalyi researched a large number of people to understand the state of flow and how it felt when someone experienced such a state. In one of his talks[10], he described that based on his studies and interviews of more than *eight thousand* people around the world – from Dominican monks, to blind nuns, to Himalayan climbers, to Navajo shepherds – who enjoy their work, regardless of the culture, regardless of education or whatever, he found that below are the seven conditions that are present when a person is in the state of flow:

1. They are completely involved in what we are doing – focused, and concentrated.
2. A sense of ecstasy – of being outside everyday reality.
3. Greater inner clarity- knowing what needs to be done, and how well we are doing.
4. Knowing that the activity is doable – that our skills are adequate to the task.

10

https://www.ted.com/talks/mihaly_csikszentmihal yi_on_flow

5. A sense of serenity- no worries about oneself, and a feeling of growing beyond the boundaries of the age.
6. Timelessness – thoroughly focused on the present, hours seem to pass by in minutes.
7. Intrinsic motivation – whatever produces flow becomes its own rewards.

If you can relate to it and even imagine such scenario, this is definitely a state of ultimate joy. The best part is that in such a state, the levels of performance undoubtedly are of the highest quality and at excitingly fast pace. That is the reason why the scientists have been trying to get deeper in the subject and examine exactly what happens inside the human brain that leads to such a state of heightened performance.

Neuroscience Tells What Happens In Brain in Flow State

As of now, scientists have made enormous progress in their research about the flow. Advancements in brain imaging technologies have allowed them to apply serious metrics on this internal state of being, which was once a subjective experience. Neuroscience has established that it can measure the state of flow in our brains by using electromyographic signals (EMF) technology.

The science behind peak human performance[11] shows that the state of flow emerges from a radical alteration in normal brain function. In flow, as attention heightens, <u>the slower and energy-expensive extrinsic system (conscious processing) is swapped out for the far faster and more efficient processing of the subconscious, intrinsic system</u>. Arne Dietrich, neuroscientist at American University of

---

[11] http://time.com/56809/the-science-of-peak-human-performance/

Beirut, who helped discover this phenomena of transition stated this as an *efficiency exchange.* He states, "We're trading energy usually used for higher cognitive functions for heightened attention and awareness."

The technical term for this efficiency exchange is *"transient hypofrontality,"* with "hypo" (meaning slow) (being the opposite of "hyper" (i.e., fast)) and "frontal" referring to the prefrontal cortex, the part of our brain that houses our higher cognitive functions. This is one of the main reasons flow feels flowy—because any brain structure that would hamper rapid-fire decision-making is literally shut off.

More precisely, three specific internal changes have been noted by neuroscientist in this:

1. **De-activation of Dorsolateral Prefrontal Cortex:** In 2008, for example, Dr. Charles Limb, a surgeon and neuroscientist used Functional Magnetic

Resonance Imaging (fMRI) to examine the brains of improv jazz musicians in flow. He found the dorsolateral prefrontal cortex (DLPFC), an area of the brain best known for self-monitoring, deactivated. Self-monitoring is the voice of doubt, also known as our inner critic – the worst enemy. Since flow is a fluid state—where problem solving is nearly automatic—second guessing can only slow down that process. When the DLPFC goes silent, the source of origin of self-doubt or second-guessing shuts off. The result is the state of liberation. We act without hesitation. Creativity becomes more free-flowing, risk taking becomes less fearful, and the combination lets us flow at a far faster clip. It is pertinent to note here that cardio exercise re-directs blood flow far away from the DLPFC to the motor parts of the brain, enabling a more embodied focus without interference from self-consciousness, distraction or negative thinking.

2. **Change in the brainwaves:** Not only DLPFC gets quiet, but in the state of flow, the function of our brainwaves changes. In the state of flow, we shift from the fast-moving beta waves (frequency of 12 to 38 Hz) of waking consciousness down to the far slower borderline between alpha and theta (8Hz and below). Alpha is day-dreaming mode—when we slip from idea to idea without much internal resistance. Theta, meanwhile, only shows up during rapid eye movement (REM) sleep or just before we fall asleep, in that hypnogogic gap where ideas combine in truly radical ways. Theta is our gateway to learning, memory, and intuition. In theta, our senses are withdrawn from the external world and focused on signals originating from within.

These slower brainwaves help us to get the maximum benefits of our cognitive abilities and speed up our decisions making process.

3. **Release of pleasure-inducing neurochemicals:** Besides above two changes i.e. quieting of DLFPC and change

in the brainwaves, finally, there's a neurochemistry of flow. A team of neuroscientists at Bonn University in Germany discovered that endorphins are released during the state of flow. Also, other researchers have determined that additionally brain releases other chemicals like norepinephrine, dopamine, anandamide, and serotonin in the state of flow. All of these five components are pleasure-inducing, performance-enhancing neurochemicals, upping everything from muscle reaction times to attention, pattern recognition and lateral thinking—the three horsemen of rapid-fire problem-solving.

Taken together, all of these above changes in brain function provided the scientists with an exceptionally potent workaround for the problem of teaching people how to be more creative. Instead of finding some outside stimulants or circumstances to address this question, we can instead train up people's ability to find flow and the state's neurobiology takes care of the rest.

Researchers have already credited flow with most athletic gold medals and world championships, major scientific breakthroughs and significant progress in the arts.

In a 10-year McKinsey study[12], top executives reported being five times more productive in flow. You can focus better, because the inner critic gets silent and nothing can distract you in that state of flow, as your inner critic shuts off, as we just learnt above.

How to Experience More Of State Of Flow

All of the above sounds great, isn't it?

By harnessing our brain's power and with the play of neurochemistry and transition of brainwaves, it becomes so flowy – and one can perform at heightened levels for longer hours.

---

[12] https://www.mckinsey.com/business-functions/organization/our-insights/increasing-the-meaning-quotient-of-work

But imagine yourself having gotten into that state of flow and performing at your best for a moment. How does that feel? I can tell you that experiencing the state of flow is like bliss. It is a stage where you get amazed about your potential. I have had some experienceswhile writing books that I start wondering why my typing speed was so slow – even though I type at a reasonably fast speed. That's because the ideas started showing up in my mind at exceedingly fast pace during those times. But I am not that blessed to say that I regularly experience such state. Though I wish, as everyone does; to be in such a wonderful state of flow for long period, and my practice is on to get more and more of such instances.

The techniques stated throughout in the book will help you to change your self-image, train your mental muscles to focus on what's important and with enhanced willpower, it is possible for everyone to get immersed in his work, which may lead at time to the flow state experience.

Also, through some small changes in your routines and environment, and with practice you can enhance your possibility of being in the state of flow more often. Leo Babauta, a blogger at zenhabits.net beautifully states certain steps[13] that can help you to achieve this state of flow with practice, as below:

1. **Choose work you love**. If you dread a task, you'll have a hard time losing yourself in it. If your job is made up of stuff you hate, you might want to consider finding another job. Or consider seeking projects you love to do within your current job. At any rate, be sure that whatever task you choose is something you can be passionate about.

2. **Choose an important task**. There's work you love that's easy and

---

[13] https://zenhabits.net/guide-to-achieving-flow-and-happiness-in-your-work/

unimportant, and then there's work you love that will make a long-term impact on your career and life. Choose the latter, as it will be a much better use of your time, and you can get into a state of flow.

3. **Make sure it's challenging, but not too hard**. If a task is too easy, you will be able to complete it without much thought or effort. A task should be challenging enough to require your full concentration. However, if it is too hard, you will find it difficult to lose yourself in it, as you will spend most of your concentration just trying to figure out how to do it. It may take some trial and error to find tasks of the appropriate level of difficulty.

4. **Find your quiet, peak time**. First, you'll want to find a time that's quiet, or you'll never be able to focus. That might be early morning, when you just wake, or early in the work day, when most people haven't

arrived yet or are still getting their coffee and settling down. Or you might try the lunch hour, when people are usually out of the office. Evenings work well too for many people. Or, if you're lucky, you can do it at any time of the day if you can find a quiet spot to work in. Whatever time you choose, it should also be a peak energy time for you. Find a time when you have lots of energy and can concentrate.

5. **Clear away distractions**. Aside from finding a quiet time and place to work, you'll want to clear away all other distractions. That means turning off distracting music (unless you find music that helps you focus), turning off phones, email and Facebook, Twitter notifications, and anything else that might pop up or make noise to interrupt your thoughts.

6. **Learn to focus on that task for as long as possible**. This takes

practice. You need to start on your chosen task and keep your focus on it for as long as you can. At first, many people will have difficulty, if they're used to constantly switching between tasks. But keep trying and keep bringing your focus back to your task. You'll get better. And if you can keep your focus on that task, with no distractions, and if your task has been chosen well (something you love, something important, and something challenging), you would find yourself lost yourself in flow soon.

7. **Keep practicing**. Again, this takes practice. Each step will take some practice, from finding a quiet, peak time for yourself, to clearing distractions, to choosing the right task. And especially keeping your focus on a task for a long time. But each time you fail, try to learn from it. Each time you succeed, you should also learn from it — what did

you do right? And the more you practice, the better you'll get.

8. **Reap the rewards**. Aside from the pleasure of getting into Flow, you'll also be happier with your work overall. You'll get important stuff done. You'll complete stuff more often, rather than starting and stopping frequently. All of this is hugely satisfying and rewarding. Take the time to appreciate this, and to continue to practice it every day.

Closing Thoughts

****

"Leaders set high standards. Refuse to tolerate mediocrity or poor performance." ~ Brian Tracy

Congratulations!

I appreciate your sincerity and dedication that you have shown to yourself finishing this book. Honestly, most people start the book, read through some pages and then leave it without finishing, but you are not amongst those. It shows that you care about your purpose – it means you value performing at your best levels and for sustainable period.

I sincerely hope that this book has given you enough principles and the practical strategies to attain the expertise in any skill and perform at their best levels. You know there are no outside factors that stop you from reaching to you best potential. In fact, psychology and neuroscience have already shown you the vast potential of the human body and mind. There is nothing that is required from outside, you have everything within yourself to enhance your level of performance and achieve any heights you choose for yourself through deliberate practice.

Therefore, I urge you not to let this knowledge wither away by non-action and the passage of time. It is you who can turn this knowledge into your personal wisdom to lead your best possible life.

Someone said, "Knowledge is power"

But this is not entirely true. Knowledge is only a potential power. The real power emerges when you apply the acquired knowledge to form definite plans of action married with the definiteness of your purpose.

You don't need to do it all at once. Just pick one strategy or practice today and start imbibing into your daily life. The principles, you have been exposed to in this book – you know are already implemented by high-achievers- so they work. Therefore, they will work for you too. You just need to be intentional and take action.

I wish you a life of mastery and excellence in all your pursuits.

Cheers

Som Bathla

Your Free Gift Bundle:

Did you download your Gift Bundle already?

Click and Download your Free Gift Bundle Below

Claim Your Gift Bundle!

Three AMAZING BOOKS for FREE on:

1. Mind Hacking - in just 21 days!
2. Time Hacking- How to Cheat Time!
3. The Productivity Manifesto

Download Now

You can also download your gift at http://sombathla.com/freegiftbundle

DISCLAIMER

While all attempts have been made to verify the information provided in this publication, the author does not assume any responsibility for errors, omissions, or contrary interpretations of the subject matter herein.

The views expressed are those of the author alone, and should not be taken as expert instruction or commands. The reader is responsible for his or her own actions.

The author makes no representations or warranties with respect to the accuracy or completeness of the contents of this work and specifically disclaims all warranties, including without limitation warranties of fitness for a particular purpose. No